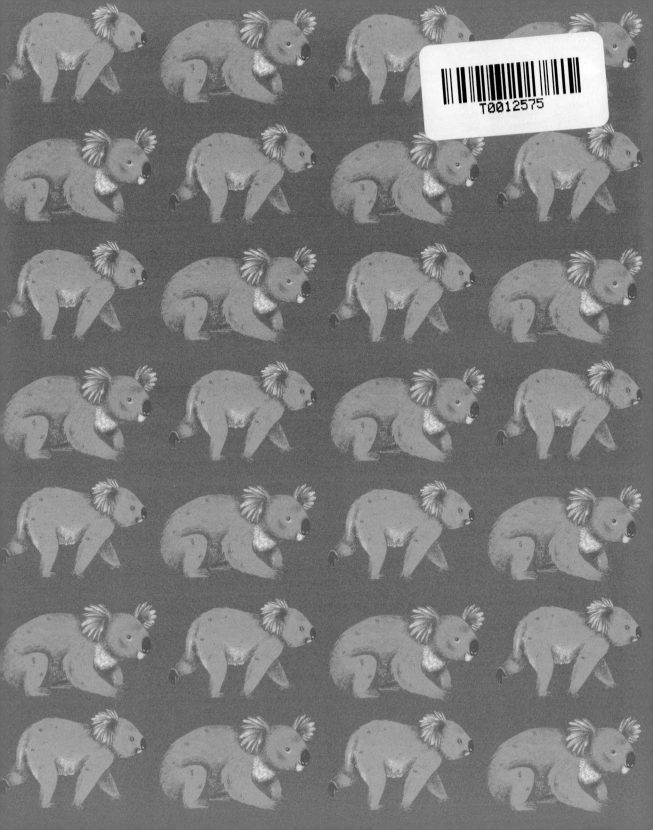

YOUNG ZOOLOGIST
KOALA

A FIRST FIELD GUIDE TO THE CUDDLY
MARSUPIAL FROM AUSTRALIA

CONTENTS

HELLO, YOUNG ZOOLOGIST!

My name is Professor Chris Daniels. I am an Australian zoologist and your personal guide as we explore the world of the koala. I study koalas and work with others to save them from extinction. Koalas are wonderful and very different from all other animals. They live in the forests of Australia but in some places, like my hometown of Adelaide, you can spot them on neighborhood streets and even in people's backyards! Let's explore their world together—you'll soon understand why they are one of the world's most loved animals.

PROFESSOR CHRIS DANIELS

FACT FILE

SCIENTIFIC NAME
Phascolarctos cinereus

GROUP
Marsupials

LOCATION IN AUSTRALIA

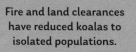

Fire and land clearances have reduced koalas to isolated populations.

The dark green areas on the map are where koalas live.

EATS
About 20 different species of eucalyptus tree

NAME
Koala means "no drink" in the Dharug language.

HABITAT
Forests and open woodlands of Australia

CLASS
Mammal

LIFE SPAN
12–15 years

SUBSPECIES
These koalas look different, but they both belong to the same species.

The large brown koala is found in Victoria and South Australia.

The northern subspecies is found in Queensland and New South Wales.

CONSERVATION STATUS
Endangered. Declining in the north (Queensland and New South Wales), but common or abundant in parts of the south (Victoria and South Australia).

BEFORE YOU GET STARTED

Always carry a notebook and pencils to write down everything you see!

1 FLAG AND BAG

Capturing koalas using the "flag and bag" technique involves holding a red rag connected to a pole above a koala's face. The koala then backs down the tree and can be safely caught in the bag.

2 NOTEBOOK

Scientists use notebooks to record data such as the size, weight, body shape, and sex of koalas. This information is vital and is always recorded for every animal.

3 MEASURING EQUIPMENT

Callipers are used to measure the body proportions of animals. Other important field equipment includes scales and tape measures. It's important to pack field equipment in a waterproof bag—it often rains in forests!

Scientists catch and measure koalas for many reasons, including to discover where they go, what they eat, and how healthy they are. It's important that scientists come prepared with the right equipment to study the koalas.

4

6

A drone is an uncrewed aircraft that can be remotely controlled. It has sensors to prevent crashes.

In the Australian wildfires of 2020, rescuers used a dog named Bear to find injured koalas.

5

4 RADIO COLLAR
In the wild, scientists capture koalas and fit them with radio collars before releasing them and tracking their movements. Radio collars give out signals that can be detected up to 330 ft (100 m) away.

5 DOG TRACKER
Another method of finding koalas involves using specially trained dogs! They can use their skills to track, find, and sniff out koalas, even ones high up in the tallest of trees.

6 DRONE
Using drones to count koalas saves time and reduces stress on the animals. Drones take pictures of the koalas' faces, because scientists can identify each individual koala by patterns on its nose.

MEET THE KOALA

GREAT HEARING

Koalas hear exceptionally well. Males attract females with a deep grunting call that travels miles through the forest. They also make sounds when distressed or when greeting each other.

NIGHT VISION

Koalas can see well in the dark. They have vertical-slit pupils, and it is not uncommon for them to have one blue eye and one brown eye. Koalas can also judge distances well, which keeps them from falling out of trees!

THUMBS-UP

Koalas have two thumbs on each hand, which they use for grabbing branches and leaves. They also have long, sharp claws and ridges on their fingers, like fingerprints. The big toes on each foot don't have claws, and they can move like thumbs. This helps koalas climb down trees backward.

Front hand

Hindfoot

Say hello to a koala! These tree-dwelling marsupials are the only surviving members of the family Phascolarctidae (meaning "pouched bear"). Their closest living relatives are wombats. Koalas eat only eucalyptus leaves and they usually live alone.

BOOPING NOSES

Koalas greet each other by touching noses, which is called booping. Their amazing sense of smell allows them to tell young and old leaves apart.

TOUGH BOTTOM

The skin on the backside of a koala is very thick and tough. This hardened rump is squeezed into the fork of tree branches and safely anchors the koala—even in very high winds.

COZY POUCH

Like all marsupials, female koalas have a pouch. They suckle one or two babies, called joeys, for about six months. The joey will ride on its mom's back for another four to six months before leaving.

ARE KOALAS BEARS?

Australians hate it when koalas are called bears! Koalas might look a little like bears, but they are not related. Both are mammals and provide milk to their young, but that's where the similarities end. Let's take a look at what makes them different.

BEARS

Bears are large, terrestrial (land-dwelling) mammals. They are found in Europe, Asia, and the Americas, but not in Australia. Different species of bear include the grizzly bear, the brown bear, and the giant panda.

Koalas are arboreal (tree-dwelling) mammals that are only found in Australia.

Koalas are a type of mammal called a marsupial.

Different bear species eat different food, including meat, fish, fruit, berries, insects, and bamboo.

WHAT IS A MARSUPIAL?

All marsupials carry their young in a pouch. Marsupial young are born as tiny, furless, jelly bean–sized babies called joeys. The joey crawls to the pouch and attaches to a teat. It drinks milk from the teat and grows to become a small version of the adult.

Kangaroo mothers keep their pouches spotlessly clean to keep the joeys healthy.

The giant koala was a third larger than the modern species.

GIANT ANCESTORS

Koalas first appeared about 25 million years ago, coinciding with the spread of the eucalyptus tree. They probably evolved from a land-dwelling, wombat-like ancestor. The giant koala is now extinct, but it remains the largest known tree-dwelling marsupial of all time. At least 18 species of koala have been identified from fossils!

MEET THE FAMILY

KOALAS AND WOMBATS

Koalas and wombats are collectively called the Vombatiformes. They were once the most dominant of all marsupials across Australia, but most died out between 50,000 and 10,000 years ago.

Only three species of wombat and one species of koala exist today.

MARSUPIAL MOLE

The only two types of marsupial mole are found in the hot, sandy deserts of central Australia. They look and behave like true moles, hunting for grubs and worms underground.

TASMANIAN DEVIL

The Tasmanian devil is the largest remaining member of the meat-eating Dasyuridae family. Restricted to the island of Tasmania, to the south of mainland Australia, the devil is known for its incredible bite and eerie howl. It is a scavenger, which means it will eat any dead animal it can find.

Marsupials originated in North America and spread to Australia about 50 million years ago. There are five groups of Australian marsupials. They range from tiny moles and bandicoots to large kangaroos and giant wombats.

KANGAROOS AND POSSUMS

There are 127 species of kangaroo and possum. All of them have two incisor teeth for chopping vegetation. Kangaroos also have toes that are fused together on their hind feet.

Kangaroos belong to the family Macropodidae, which means "big feet."

Kangaroos have long and powerful legs that allow them to jump up to 10 ft (3 m) high!

BANDICOOT

Bandicoots are vital for forest health because their digging increases nutrients in the soil. Six species became extinct because they were hunted by cats and foxes that were introduced to Australia by humans.

ATTRACTING A MATE

Koalas breed once a year and usually have one joey. Female koalas can give birth to twins, but it is pretty rare. Finding a mate is no easy task. Both male and female koalas have a few tricks up their sleeves that help them find a perfect match!

CALLING

Male koalas call from early springtime (August and September in Australia). They produce a deep, low grunt that attracts females and tells other males to stay away. Females also bellow and squeal when calling for a mate.

SCENT-MARKING

Male koalas leave their scent on trees so females know where to find them. They do this by rubbing a gland on their chest against trees. The strong-smelling, oily liquid is only produced in spring.

MATING

Females start breeding from the age of two, while males start from the age of three—but they are more successful at around the age of five. Mating occurs in late spring, with the baby born about 35 days later.

FIGHTING FOR LOVE

Koalas are usually solitary animals, but if two males meet in the breeding season they will fight for dominance! Two evenly matched males can fight viciously. Females will also fight off unwanted males.

A JOEY'S LIFE

Like all marsupials, koalas give birth to babies that are born underdeveloped. The newborns must crawl from the birth canal to the pouch without any help! There, they grow and become stronger.

THIRSTY WORK

2 Once inside the pouch, the joey will firmly hold on to one of its mother's two teats, which swells to fill its mouth. At first, koala milk is rich in sugary nutrients called carbohydrates. As the joey grows, the protein and fat in the milk increases.

BLIND JELLY BEAN

1 The joey is tiny at birth! It measures around ¾ in (2 cm) and weighs around 0.02 oz (0.5 g). It is born blind with no fur or ears, looking like a tiny pink jelly bean. To find its mother's pouch, the joey relies only on its strength and its senses of touch and smell.

3 IN THE POUCH

After about five months, the growing joey detaches from the teat and starts eating its mom's pap, a liquid kind of poop that will allow the joey to digest leaves. The mother takes care of the joey and prevents it from falling out by squeezing the muscles in her pouch.

4 RIDING ON THE BACK

When the joey is about six to seven months old, it starts to spend time outside the pouch. Initially it snuggles into its mother's belly to stay warm, but later it rides on its mother's back. Koala joeys usually stay with their mothers for a further six months.

DAILY HABITS

MUNCH MUNCH

Most koalas only eat four or five types of eucalyptus (also known as "gum trees"). Each koala has its own eucalyptus preferences, which can change with the season.

FUNNY WADDLE

Koalas walk in a strange way. A koala's bottom is higher than its back because of its large hind legs. When hurrying, koalas bound like rabbits and can achieve speeds of up to 6 mph (10 kph).

After decades of studying and observing koalas, scientists understand their daily habits very well. Koalas sleep for most of the day, but when they're awake you will usually spot them munching away on eucalyptus leaves.

ZZZZZZZ.....

Koalas eat for about five hours a day and sleep for about 15 hours to digest the leaves! Sleeping also helps them conserve their energy for the next time they need to go foraging for a meal.

SUPER SWIMMERS

Koalas are good swimmers. They use a dog-paddle stroke, propelled by their strong back legs. However, they need help from a branch or a tree to get out of the water otherwise they can drown.

GUM TREES

When they're hungry, koalas will travel long distances in search of their favorite type of eucalyptus tree. They can even tell the different gum trees apart by smell.

THE MORE THE MERRIER

Gum leaves are low in nutrition because they are mostly made up of water. So to stay healthy and get enough nutrients, koalas need to eat about 2.2 lb (1 kg) of leaves per day. That's about 50 gum trees a year!

To spot a feeding tree, look for claw marks in the bark and lots of koala poop at the base.

SPECIAL STOMACH

Koalas have a special enlarged part of their gut called a caecum. The caecum holds the bacteria that digest the leaves. Each type of gum tree requires a different bacteria to digest it.

Caecum

SMELLY POOP

Koalas produce 200 to 300 elongated, peanut-sized poops every day, and they smell of eucalyptus!

TREE-DWELLERS

Animals that live in trees are called arboreal, and animals that live on land are called terrestrial. Koalas aren't the only arboreal animals in Australia. Other animals also have their homes high up in the trees. Let's meet them!

GREATER GLIDER

The greater glider can glide up to 330 ft (100 m) from tree to tree with its arms outstretched. The skin between its front and rear legs acts as a parachute.

RINGTAIL POSSUM

There are 23 types of possum in Australia. The ringtail possum will eat eucalyptus leaves as well as blossoms, fruit, and nectar. Ringtail possums use their tails as an extra limb to hold on to branches.

MAGPIE

Magpies make huge nests out of sticks, and the father actively protects the young. In the breeding season, koalas can be swooped at and pecked by magpies if they come too close. Ouch!

LACE MONITOR

Measuring up to 6½ ft (2 m) long, lace monitors are the largest predators in the forest. They are excellent climbers and will attack eggs, baby birds, other reptiles, and even young koalas.

THREATS TO KOALAS

In 2021 the northern koala subspecies was classified as endangered.

1 **OVERBREEDING**
In Victoria and South Australia, numbers of koalas are mysteriously increasing. In some places, there are so many koalas that they have eaten all of the eucalyptus trees and now risk starving.

2 **SWIMMING POOLS**
In southern Australia, many koalas have renal disease, a condition that stops the kidneys from working properly. This forces the animals to seek water. Some are attracted to swimming pools, where they can fall in and drown.

3 **CHLAMYDIA**
Chlamydia is a bacterial infection that affects the eyes and reproductive body parts. This disease can cause koalas to go blind, become unable to reproduce, and even die. It is highly infectious and was introduced to koalas by infected sheep.

Due to infectious diseases and habitat clearances, koala numbers are declining dramatically across Australia, especially in New South Wales and Queensland. Unfortunately these are not the only threats currently facing koalas.

4 CITY LIFE

The building of new towns and cities leads to the destruction of koala habitats. Many koalas have also moved to urban areas where they come into contact with people. They can enter houses through cat flaps, which is dangerous for both humans and koalas.

5 DANGEROUS DOGS

One side effect of koalas living in towns and cities is that they can be attacked by dogs. Large male southern koalas can fight back and sometimes even injure pet dogs. Koalas also risk being run over by cars in the street.

6 HABITAT CLEARANCE

Deforestation, or the destruction of forests, is the main threat to koalas. It creates small and isolated pockets of habitat so koalas cannot move around freely. Deforestation causes koalas to lose food sources and shelter.

DANGER IN THE FOREST

CLIMATE EMERGENCY

Climate change is causing more forest fires in Australia, and they are becoming larger and larger. The hot temperatures are killing the trees that koalas need for food, and the hot weather is drying the leaves they use to get water.

DESTROYED HABITATS

In the summer of 2019/2020, around 2% of Australia was burned by huge fires. Large areas of koala habitat were lost. On Kangaroo Island in South Australia, 85% of koala forests were destroyed, resulting in the loss of more than 40,000 koala lives.

Many gum trees grow new shoots from buds hidden inside the tree that become active because of the fires.

Forest fires are a major problem for koalas. Koala fur is so dense that it will protect them to some extent, but they can still burn their hands, feet, and noses in the fires. If koalas are trapped high up in the trees, inhaling smoke is also very dangerous.

Scientists expect to see more wildfires in the coming decades.

After the 2020 fires, people sent mittens for koalas to help their hands and feet heal.

A NEW HOPE

In 2020, Cleland Wildlife Park and the Koala Life Foundation rescued 28 fire orphans from Kangaroo Island. In two years, these koalas have had nine babies, who will help the population recover!

MYTHS AND LEGENDS

Australians love making up stories about koalas to trick visitors. There are more myths about koalas than about any other marsupial. Some stories are simply incorrect explanations for their unusual behavior!

KILLER KOALA

One myth is about killer koalas called drop bears. Supposedly they attack non-Australians by dropping onto them and biting them with their long, sharp fangs. The myth recommends smearing Vegemite, a food spread, behind your ears to protect yourself.

SLEEPY KOALAS

There is a myth that koalas have to sleep so much because chemicals in the eucalyptus leaves intoxicate them, so koalas are always drunk! This is not true. Koalas sleep to aid digestion.

Eucalyptus leaves contain toxins, but koalas can break them down in their stomachs.

KOALAS DO DRINK

The idea that koalas never drink water is false. They get most water from their food, by eating leaves. Koalas will also lick water from tree trunks or drink from water provided by humans on hot days.

GLOSSARY

Ancestor
An early type of animal from which others have evolved.

Arboreal
Tree-dwelling. An animal that lives in trees.

Breeding
Mating leading to the production of babies.

Climate change
Long-term shifts in temperature and weather patterns that occur either naturally or because they've been caused by humans.

Deforestation
The removal of a forest so the land can be used for other functions.

Eucalyptus
A type of fast-growing evergreen tree native to Australia. Koalas eat eucalyptus leaves.

Evolution
Changes over a long period of time in the way species look or behave in order to better suit the environment they live in.

Feeding tree
A specific type of eucalyptus that koalas like to eat.

Gum trees
Australian slang term for eucalyptus trees.

Habitat
The natural home or environment of an animal.

Joey
A baby or young marsupial.

Mammal
A warm-blooded, hairy or furry animal that produces milk to feed its young.

Marsupial
A type of mammal that carries and feeds its young in a pouch.

Mating
The act between a male and a female that leads to the production of babies.

Nutrients
Substances in food eaten by animals that support their life and growth.

Pouch
A pocket of skin that holds a joey as it feeds and grows. All female marsupials have pouches.

Predator
A species of animal that eats other animals.

Terrestrial
Land-dwelling. An animal that lives on the surface of the ground.

Zoologist
A scientist who studies animals.

INDEX

This has been a

NEON SQUID

production

Koalas need your help. They are now classified as endangered throughout much of their range. Help us save the koalas by donating to Koala Life. Koala Life is a not-for-profit research foundation dedicated to understanding koalas in order to protect them and their forest habitats. Visit www.koalalife.asn.au to find out more.

Author: Professor Chris Daniels
Illustrator: Marianne Lock

Editorial Assistant: Malu Rocha
US Editor: Allison Singer-Kushnir
Proofreader: Georgina Coles

Here are a view places you can see koalas in zoos:

Calgary Zoo (Alberta, Canada)

Cleveland Metroparks Zoo (Ohio)

Columbus Zoo and Aquarium (Ohio)

Los Angeles Zoo (California)

Palm Beach Zoo (Florida)

Riverbanks Zoo & Garden (South Carolina)

San Diego Zoo (California)

San Francisco Zoo & Gardens (California)

Zoo Tampa at Lowry Park (Florida)

Zoo Miami (Florida)

Copyright © 2023 St. Martin's Press
120 Broadway, New York, NY 10271

Created for St. Martin's Press
by Neon Squid
The Stables, 4 Crinan Street,
London, N1 9XW

EU representative: Macmillan Publishers Ireland Ltd,
1st Floor, The Liffey Trust Centre,
117–126 Sheriff Street Upper,
Dublin 1, D01 YC43

10 9 8 7 6 5 4 3 2 1

The right of Professor Chris Daniels to be identified as the author of this work has been asserted in accordance with the Copyright, Designs and Patents Act, 1988.

Library of Congress Cataloging-in-Publication Data is available.

Printed and bound by Vivar Printing in Malaysia.

ISBN: 978-1-684-49283-1

Published in January 2023.

www.neonsquidbooks.com